AF228585

— OUTDOOR ADVENTURES —

MOUNTAIN BIKING

By Christa C. Hogan

SportsZone

An Imprint of Abdo Publishing
abdobooks.com

abdobooks.com

Published by Abdo Publishing, a division of ABDO, PO Box 398166, Minneapolis, Minnesota 55439. Copyright © 2020 by Abdo Consulting Group, Inc. International copyrights reserved in all countries. No part of this book may be reproduced in any form without written permission from the publisher. SportsZone™ is a trademark and logo of Abdo Publishing.

Printed in the United States of America, North Mankato, Minnesota
092019
012020

Cover Photo: iStockphoto
Interior Photos: Maciej Kopaniecki/Shutterstock Images, 5, 31; Fox Photos/ Hulton Archive/Getty Images, 6; Monkey Business Images/iStockphoto, 9; Ruslan Dashinsky/iStockphoto, 11; Maxim Petrichuk/Shutterstock Images, 12; Yuri Hoyda/Shutterstock Images, 15, 28; Auriga Design/iStockphoto, 16; Science & Society Picture Library/Getty Images, 19; Olena Mykhaylova/Shutterstock Images, 20; iStockphoto, 23, 36, 39; Shutterstock Images, 24, 27, 32; Wave Break Media/Shutterstock Images, 35; Kyle T. Perry/Shutterstock Images, 41; Juanan Barros Moreno/Shutterstock Images, 43; Colton Stiffler/Shutterstock Images, 44

Editor: Patrick Donnelly
Series Designer: Colleen McLaren

Library of Congress Control Number: 2019941985

Publisher's Cataloging-in-Publication Data

Names: Hogan, Christa C., author
Title: Mountain Biking / by Christa C. Hogan
Description: Minneapolis, Minnesota : Abdo Publishing, 2020 | Series: Outdoor adventures | Includes online resources and index.
Identifiers: ISBN 9781532190513 (lib. bdg.) | ISBN 9781532176364 (ebook)
Subjects: LCSH: Mountain biking--Juvenile literature. | Off-road biking--Juvenile literature. | All terrain biking--Juvenile literature. | Cycling--Juvenile literature. | Extreme sports--Juvenile literature. | Outdoor recreation--Juvenile literature
Classification: DDC 796.63--dc23

TABLE OF
CONTENTS

CHAPTER 1

EVOLUTION OF MOUNTAIN BIKING

A thin dirt trail cuts through the forest. Rocks and roots jut from the ground. The mountain biker leans over his handlebars. He adjusts his weight in the seat. Other mountain bikers disappear into the trees ahead of him. He pedals faster.

Suddenly, the trees part. The biker has reached the top of the mountain. He brakes. Dirt and pebbles fly up behind him. He climbs off his bike and joins his friends. They admire the mountain view while they catch their breath. Then they hop back on their bikes. More adventures await.

Explorers can reach beautiful vistas on their mountain bikes.

English cross-country bikers make their way through an obstacle in the 1930s.

Mountain biking is a popular pastime. Mountain bikers don't ride on paved roads. They ride over rough terrain, such as mountain trails. They use bikes with special features. These features make mountain bikes perfect for riding off road.

Mountain bikers can ride alone or with groups. They may also participate in races and competitions. Mountain bikers enjoy being outdoors and staying fit.

THE HISTORY OF MOUNTAIN BIKING

Mountain biking has been around since the 1800s. Back then, few roads were paved. Cyclists rode on dirt roads and trails instead. However, some riders took traditional cycling to a new level.

In 1897 the 25th Infantry Bicycle Corps rode from Fort Missoula in Montana to St. Louis, Missouri. The 41-day journey covered 1,900 miles (3,000 km) of mountains, streams, and deserts. Riding bikes helped them cover twice as much ground as they would have on foot or horseback.

In the 1950s, the Velo Cross Club Parisien organized the earliest mountain biking races. Twenty young bicycle enthusiasts made adaptations to their bikes

WITNESSING HISTORY

Each year, thousands of mountain bikers visit the Marin Museum of Bicycling and the Mountain Bike Hall of Fame in Fairfax, California. The museum has a collection of bikes that spans almost 200 years. Visitors can learn about mountain biking history and the cyclists who made it possible.

to better handle rough terrain. The group rode their bikes on motocross racetracks.

During the 1960s and 1970s, other cycling groups popped up in California. Each group helped popularize the sport. The adventures of groups such as the Larkspur Canyon Gang inspired a new generation of mountain bikers. The Cupertino Riders' bikes included gearshifts and brakes that are still used on bikes today.

By the 1980s and 1990s, mountain bikes had advanced features. They included reinforced tires, heavy-duty suspensions, lightweight frames, and interchangeable gears. Mountain bikes were made from more durable materials that helped their riders handle all terrain.

THE FUTURE OF MOUNTAIN BIKING

Mountain biking is a mainstream sport today. More than 40 million Americans participate in mountain biking each year. It's one of the most popular outdoor trail activities in the United States.

Mountain bikers have forged new trails across generations. Their innovations have improved on old technology. Mountain biking today is a reflection of these riders. The sport will continue to change as today's mountain bikers determine its future.

CHAPTER 2

TYPES OF MOUNTAIN BIKING

Mountain biking is about more than just riding a bike off road. A lot goes into choosing the proper bike and equipment. Cyclists learn special riding techniques to perform better on the trails. Cyclists also follow guidelines for safety and nature conservation.

First though, new riders should know that there are many different kinds of mountain biking. Knowing the differences between these styles can open new possibilities. Then riders can also better prepare themselves and select the best equipment.

Mountain biking takes place on all types of terrain.

Technical trails might take riders across streams or standing water.

TRAIL RIDING

Trail riding is the most common type of mountain biking. Mountain biking trails often cut through rugged terrain such as hills, streams, forests, and fields.

Bike trails are marked by skill level. Trails are noted as beginner, intermediate, expert, or double expert.

New mountain bikers use beginner trails to gain experience. Once they master beginner trails, riders move on to more difficult challenges. To use them safely, expert trails require professional-level skills.

Trails also can be technical or freeride. Technical trails have more difficult features. These trails are usually a single track and fit only one rider. Technical trails might also have heavy roots and rocks, steep hills, water crossings, or jumps.

Freeride trails are double-track trails. These trails can accommodate two cyclists side by side. Freeride trails are often designed to be ridden downhill. Both types of trails can feature engineered elements such as bridges and embankments.

BIKE SKILLS AND TERRAIN PARKS

Cyclists can build their confidence in skills parks and terrain parks. Skills parks feature obstacles such as elevated bridges, jumps, and dirt hills. Terrain parks are located at off-season ski resorts, abandoned logging roads, or even urban overpasses. Both types of parks help riders practice for trail riding.

CROSS-COUNTRY

Cross-country riders also use trails. However, they tend to ride longer distances. They also prefer more challenging climbs and focus on speed. Cross-country rides can vary from a few miles to 25 miles (40 km) or more.

ALL-MOUNTAIN OR ENDURO

All-mountain or enduro riders look for bigger climbs and steep drops. The word *enduro* is a racing term. Enduro riders race to see who can reach the bottom of a mountain the fastest. Enduro bikes tend to be lightweight for climbing but sturdy for trickier descents.

Terrain parks give bikers a chance to practice their skills in a controlled environment.

DOWNHILL

Downhill biking is all about getting to the bottom of a trail fast. Trails are accessed by lifts. Lifts are often found at off-season ski resorts. Riders use heavy bikes that can take a beating. They also wear full-face helmets. Body armor protects them during falls. Downhill bikers don't have to pedal much.

However, they need to make quick decisions to tackle fast-changing, rough terrain.

FAT BIKING

Bikes with extra-wide tires help bikers tackle challenging terrain, such as snow or sand. Fat biking also takes place on regular mountain biking trails. The wide tires are great for covering a variety of terrains. Fat bikes are well balanced, which makes them a good choice for beginning mountain bikers.

There are as many different types of mountain biking as there are riders and terrains. Which style riders choose depends on their tastes and location. Every style has something exciting to offer.

Fat bikes excel on soft terrain such as sand or snow.

CHAPTER 3

ALL ABOUT THE BIKE

Bikes have come a long way since they were first made in the 1800s. German baron Karl von Drais is considered the father of the bicycle. His first bike was called the velocipede. This bike didn't have a chain, brakes, or pedals. Riders used their feet to push off the ground to create motion.

John Kemp Starley improved on Drais's design in 1885. Starley's Rover Safety Bicycle looked more like our bikes today. The safety bike had a diamond-shaped metal frame. The bike also had two equal-sized wheels. It used pedals and a chain system to move the rear tire. However, these bikes

John Kemp Starley helped modernize bicycle design in the late 1800s.

19

Many features of the modern mountain bike help riders navigate through rough terrain.

were so rough to ride that they were nicknamed "boneshakers."

Early mountain bikes were created by cycling enthusiasts. They added fatter tires and more suspension to traditional bikes. The first modern mountain bikes were hand built by Joe Breeze in the late 1970s. His mountain bikes featured sturdy yet lightweight frames. Other improvements quickly followed.

Today mountain bikes look very different from road bikes. Their handlebars are flat, low, and wide for improved cornering. Knobby tires help riders navigate narrow dirt trails. Frames are often made of aluminum or carbon fiber and are solid yet light. Shock absorbers and suspension forks smooth out bumpy rides.

CHOOSING A MOUNTAIN BIKE

Mountain bikes come in small, medium, and large sizes. Finding a proper-fitting bike is essential for every mountain biker. A bicycle shop can help new riders choose the bike that works best for their body type and height. A test ride can also give riders a feel for how the bike handles.

Riders can choose from several kinds of mountain bikes. Options include hardtail and full suspension.

Selecting the right mountain bike depends on the rider. Different styles of riding require different kinds of bikes and parts.

HARDTAIL SUSPENSION

Hardtail bikes offer suspension only on the front tire. Suspension helps absorb the shock of riding over obstacles such as large rocks. Hardtail bikes usually have fork suspensions. Hardtail bikes weigh less than bikes with full suspensions and tend to cost less. They also require less maintenance. Hardtail bikes work well on pavement, smooth trails, and hills.

FULL SUSPENSION

Full-suspension bikes offer suspension on both the front and back tires. Full-suspension bikes tend to be heavier and cost more. They also require more maintenance. However, full-suspension bikes are great for cross-country rides and more advanced and steep trails.

— KNOW YOUR BIKE —

The typical mountain bike includes many important parts.

RIGID

Rigid bikes lack any suspension, so they are lighter. Rigid bikes are also less expensive and easier to maintain. Rigid bikes often use fat tires with low tire pressure. The squishy tires absorb the bumps and jolts of trails.

Hardtail bikes feature front-fork suspensions but no suspension on the back tire.

WHEELS

Wheels come in several widths and heights. Wide or fat tires provide riders with more stability on rough trails. Wide tires also offer traction in sand or snow and a smoother ride. Tall wheels help cross-country riders cover more ground quickly. Short wheels are more responsive and easier to steer.

GEARS

Shifting or changing gears helps riders climb steep hills more easily. Mountain bikes come with thumb or grip shifters that change gears. Mountain bikes can have as few as one gear or as many as 30 gears. Bikes used for downhill or flat trails need fewer gears.

PEDALS

Pedals on mountain bikes come in either platform or clipless styles. Platform pedals are a good choice for beginner riders. The riders' shoes aren't attached to the pedals' flat surface. That allows riders to quickly put a foot down to maintain their balance.

Clipless pedals attach to the cleats of special bike shoes. Clipless pedals give riders more power and reduce stress on riders' knees and hips. However, it takes practice to unclip quickly when needed.

CHAPTER 4

RIDING FOR BEGINNERS

Making the change from riding on pavement to riding over streams and boulders takes practice. Mountain bikers use special techniques to tackle the diverse challenges of off-road terrain. They also ride differently than when they're on paved trails. Beginners can practice in level, grassy areas before tackling trails.

POSITIONING

Mountain bikers sit in either a neutral or attack position. When riding smooth or flat trails, they use a neutral position. Their body weight rests evenly

A racer leans into the attack position.

TRANSROCKIES
54
27

Mountain bikers lean into the turn while cornering at high speeds.

between the front and back tires. Their elbows are bent. The pedals are level. The neutral body position allows riders to remain alert but relaxed.

With steep or rocky trails, mountain bikers move into the attack position. They increase the bend in their knees and elbows. This shifts their weight over the handlebars. They also hover off the seat and lean their hips back. The attack position allows riders to make constant adjustments to stay balanced.

STEERING AND CORNERING

Mountain bikers keep their gaze focused ahead on the trail. This helps them spot obstacles in time to adjust their course. When they find a clear path around an obstacle, they can avoid jerking the handlebars and make smooth turns instead. They also keep their grip light on the handlebars and lean forward to improve traction.

When cornering, riders look ahead to the end of the turn. They also keep their head and shoulders pointed in the direction they want to go. When riding at higher speeds, they lean into the turn instead of steering sharply. This allows the rider to maintain better control of the bike.

BRAKING

Mountain bikes use hand levers. The levers operate brakes for the front and back tires. To brake, riders squeeze the levers evenly and smoothly. Too much pressure on the front brake could send the rider over the handlebars. Too much pressure on the back brake could result in a skid.

During a skid, it takes longer for the bike to stop, and the rider can lose control. Skidding also damages trails and the natural environment. So it's best to maintain even pressure on both hand levers.

FALLING

Falls happen, especially for new riders. When falling, many new riders try to catch themselves. However, this can lead to broken wrists and arms. Experienced riders learn to keep their arms in close to their body as they fall.

Falling is a common part of mountain biking. Riders can practice reacting before it happens. They can practice twisting the handlebars as they fall. The handlebars often catch the weight of the impact.

Riders can also practice jumping or stepping off as the bike falls.

OTHER TIPS

Experienced mountain bikers "stay loose" when they ride. They let the bike do all the work. They hover over the seat when trails get bumpy, and when

descending, they flare out their arms and legs to let the bike move.

Mountain bikers say that momentum is their friend. They keep moving forward at a steady speed. Momentum helps the bike conquer more technical terrain.

Finally, experienced mountain bikers use their weight. When climbing steep inclines, they shift their weight over the handlebars. This provides greater traction to the front tire. On steep declines, riders lean back. They shift their weight to the back tire to prevent going over the handlebars.

Riders adjust their body weight to adapt to changing terrain.

CHAPTER 5

SAFETY AND RESPONSIBLE RIDING

Mountain biking is a sport for the adventurous. It can also be dangerous. That's why mountain bikers take precautions to stay safe.

HELMETS

Helmets protect mountain bikers' heads during falls. Some trails and parks require helmets. Helmets have hard outer shells and padding inside. Riders secure their helmets with a strap under the chin.

A helmet's chin strap is adjustable to allow for the best fit.

35

Mountain bike helmets differ from road bike helmets. Mountain bike helmets have visors and offer additional protection at the back. Helmets worn by downhill bikers include a full face mask.

The right helmet will fit snug but not tight. The helmet will rest level, one inch above the brow. The helmet should not shift from side to side or front to back. Helmets that are involved in a crash should be replaced. Otherwise, helmets need to be replaced every five years or when they no longer fit.

PADS

Some mountain bikers also wear pads and body armor. Trail riders may wear flexible knee or elbow pads. Enduro riders wear heavier padding. Downhill racers add shin guards. Pads protect riders from injury during a fall.

GET INVOLVED

Mountain bike trails are often built and maintained by volunteers. Joining a local mountain biking organization is a great way to get involved. Volunteers remove fallen branches and build new obstacles. Volunteers keep trails safe and fun for everyone.

BIKE CHECK

Riders check their bikes before hitting the trails. They ensure tires are properly inflated. They check that the front and back brakes work. They also lubricate their chains. Safety checks prevent accidents and help bikes last longer.

RESPONSIBLE RIDING

Mountain bikers are a diverse community. They have different skill levels and engage in different types of biking. However, there are a few guidelines all mountain bikers try to follow. These rules ensure that mountain biking is fun for everyone. The rules also protect the environment and keep riders safe.

Stick to the trail—Mountain bikers use existing trails. Riding outside the trails damages the local environment. They ride single file down single-track trails. They also walk over an obstacle instead of riding around it. Riding around obstacles is called *braiding*. Braiding trails causes soil erosion. Mountain bikers avoid riding in muddy areas because it can create ruts. They ride through standing water and not around it. Caring for trails keeps the trails open to riders for years to come. Riding on posted trails also protects riders from injuries.

Be considerate—Mountain bike trails can be shared with wildlife, hikers, and horses. Mountain bikers yield to all three. Descending riders also give way to those who are climbing up a trail. Riders are courteous to other mountain bikers too. When passing another mountain biker, riders slow down. They ring a bell or announce themselves. They wait for the person ahead of them to move aside before passing.

On a single-track trail, mountain bikers should always ride single file.

Be safe—Mountain bikers plan ahead for their rides. They pack maps and supplies for the day. They carry first aid and repair kits. They ride with a friend. If riding alone, they let someone else know where they are going in case they get hurt or lost.

Leave no trace—Mountain bikers conserve nature. To protect the environment, they try to follow the philosophy of "Leave No Trace." This means not littering or causing damage to the landscape. Responsible mountain bikers also never ride on land that is protected for conservation.

These rules keep mountain bikers safe. The rules protect the environment. They also help maintain trails for future riders.

MOUNTAIN BIKING ADVENTURES

Once riders master the basics, they can look forward to many different experiences. Stunning mountain trails, fast-paced enduro races, adrenaline-pumping downhills—options for mountain bike adventures are endless.

TRAILS

Trails such as the Whole Enchilada Trail in Moab, Utah, are a nature lover's dream. The trail winds through aspen glades and the Porcupine Rim. Riders also get jaw-dropping views of red-rock desert and

Many parts of the western United States feature scenic bike trails.

the Colorado River. The trail is 34 miles (55 km) long with more than 7,000 feet (11,200 m) of downhill.

The 401 Trail is a 14-mile (23-km) loop located in Crested Butte, Colorado. Even experienced riders find biking at more than two miles (3.2 km) above sea level challenging. The trail climbs through miles of dense forest. At the top, however, riders get a 360-degree view of the Elk Mountains. Then they descend hillside-hugging trails through wildflower meadows. Riders flock to the 401 for some of the best alpine biking in the United States.

RACES

Some competitive bikers might join a race event. In enduro races, riders compete to descend steep,

technically challenging trails. The fastest rider wins. The Enduro World Series is the ultimate enduro racing event. Riders from around the world compete to become the best enduro racer in the world.

Cross-country racing events are also popular. Each year cross-country riders take on the Park City P2P in Utah. The race is a famous point-to-point event. Racers must be in good physical shape. They cover 75 miles (120 km), including more than 12,000 feet (3,600 m) of climbing, in nine hours or less.

Some ski hills convert to mountain bike parks in the summer.

MOUNTAIN BIKE RESORTS AND PARKS

Mountain bike resorts allow riders to experience new and exciting challenges. In winter, Snowshoe Mountain Resort in West Virginia is a ski resort. In summer, however, the resort turns into a mountain biking paradise. The resort offers two lifts up the mountain to access 40 downhill trails. Riders might not see any snow. But they will face rock gardens, gap jumps, steep slopes, big drops, and plenty of thrills.

In Mammoth Bike Park in California, riders have access to 80 miles (129 km) of single-track trails. Cross-country trails promise gorgeous views. Artificial obstacles provide an added challenge. The resort also offers lessons to help beginners improve.

Mountain biking appeals to nature lovers, thrill seekers, and cycling enthusiasts alike. The sport has grown from its humble beginnings. Mountain biking will continue to grow and change with its riders. But it will always be a great way to exercise and experience nature.

GLOSSARY

descend
To go down from a higher point to a lower point.

environment
The surroundings where a person, animal, or plant lives.

erosion
The slow destruction of a surface.

inflated
Filled with air.

maintenance
The process of keeping something in good condition.

momentum
Forward motion.

motocross
A motorcycle race over rough terrain.

obstacles
Things that block a path or prevent progress.

suspension
A system of springs and shock absorbers that cushions a bike from road conditions.

terrain
The physical features of a tract of land.

MORE INFORMATION

BOOKS

Abdo, Kenny. *Mountain Bikes*. Minneapolis, MN: Abdo, 2018.

Nixon, James. *How to Be a Mountain Biking Champion*. London, UK: Franklin Watts, 2017.

ONLINE RESOURCES

To learn more about mountain biking, please visit **abdobooklinks.com** or scan this QR code. These links are routinely monitored and updated to provide the most current information available.

INDEX

ABOUT THE AUTHOR

Christa C. Hogan lives in North Carolina with her husband and three boys. She enjoys many outdoor activities, including hiking, biking, skiing, and scuba diving.